The Seasons
SUMMER

Written by Stephanie Hedlund · Illustrated by Stephanie Bauer

magic Wagon

visit us at www.abdopublishing.com

Published by Magic Wagon, a division of the ABDO Group, PO Box 398166, Minneapolis, Minnesota 55439.

Printed in the United States of America, North Mankato, Minnesota.
052013
092013
♻ This book contains at least 10% recycled materials.

Written by Stephanie Hedlund
Illustrated by Stephanie Bauer
Edited by Rochelle Baltzer
Cover and interior layout and design by Neil Klinepier

Library of Congress Cataloging-in-Publication Data

Hedlund, Stephanie F., 1977-
  Summer / by Stephanie Hedlund ; illustrated by Stephanie Bauer.
      pages cm. -- (The seasons)
  ISBN 978-1-61641-994-3
  1. Summer--Juvenile literature. I. Bauer, Stephanie, illustrator. II. Title.
  QB637.6.H44 2014
  508.2--dc23
                        2012049768

Contents

Summer

There are four seasons during the year.
Do you know what season is third?
That's right, it is summer!
Then comes autumn, winter, and spring.

winter

spring

summer

Autumn

Why?

Earth travels around the sun during the year.
When Earth is tilted toward the sun, it is summer.
Some places feel like summer all year.
Near the **equator**, the **temperatures** are warm most of the time.

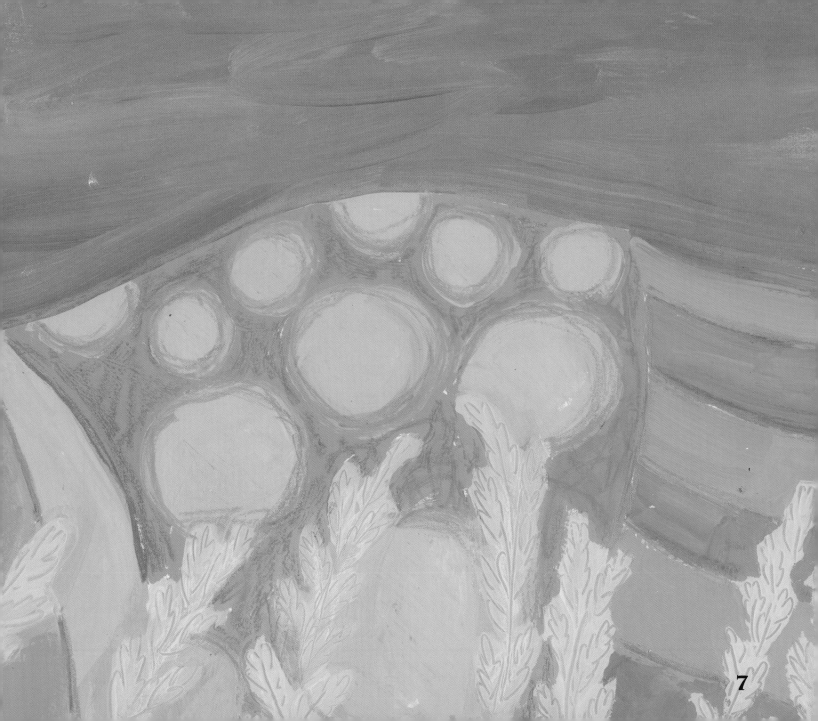

7

When?

The **summer solstice** is June 20 or 21.
That is the longest day of the year.
It is also the start of summer!

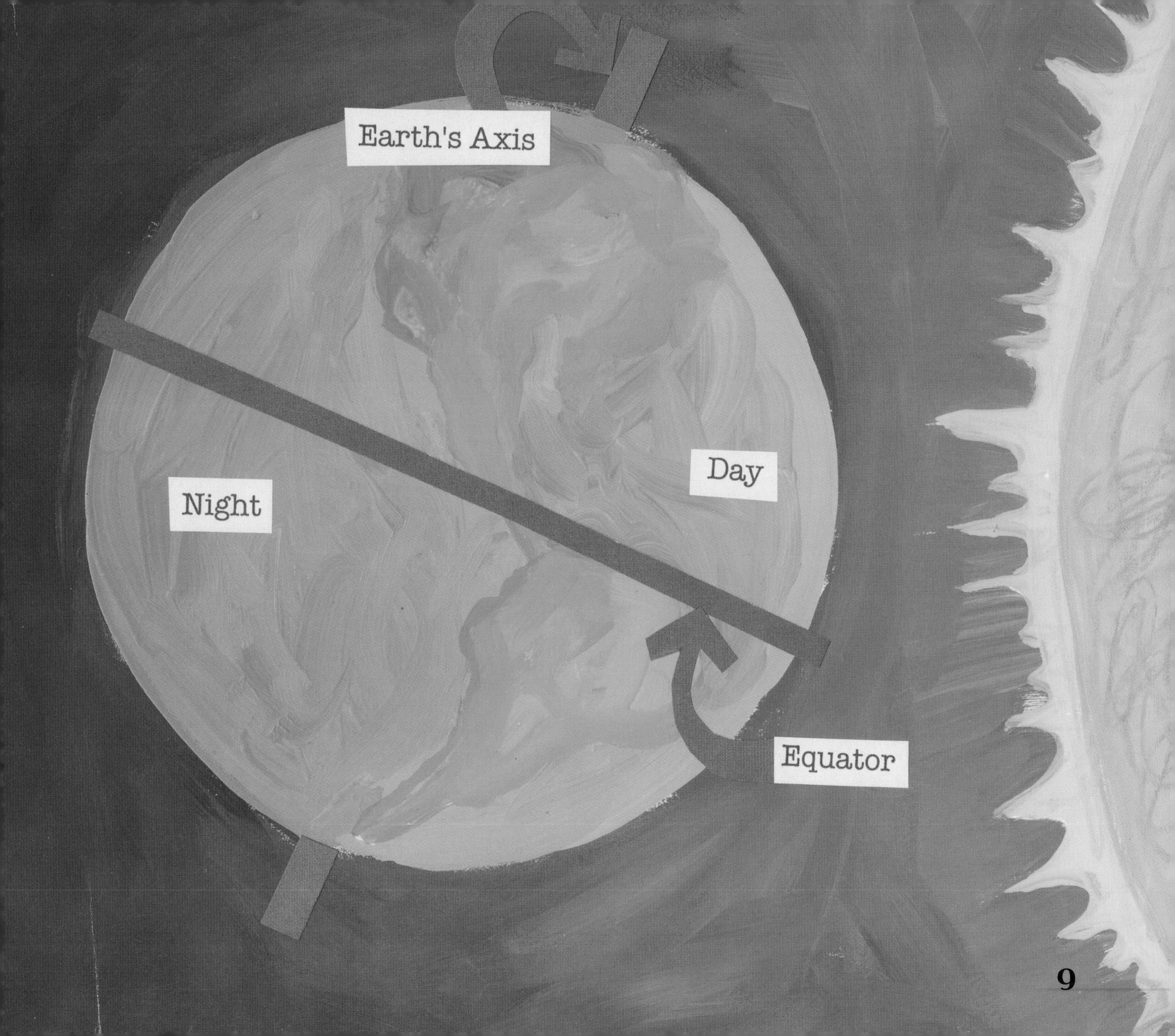

Earth's Axis

Night

Day

Equator

9

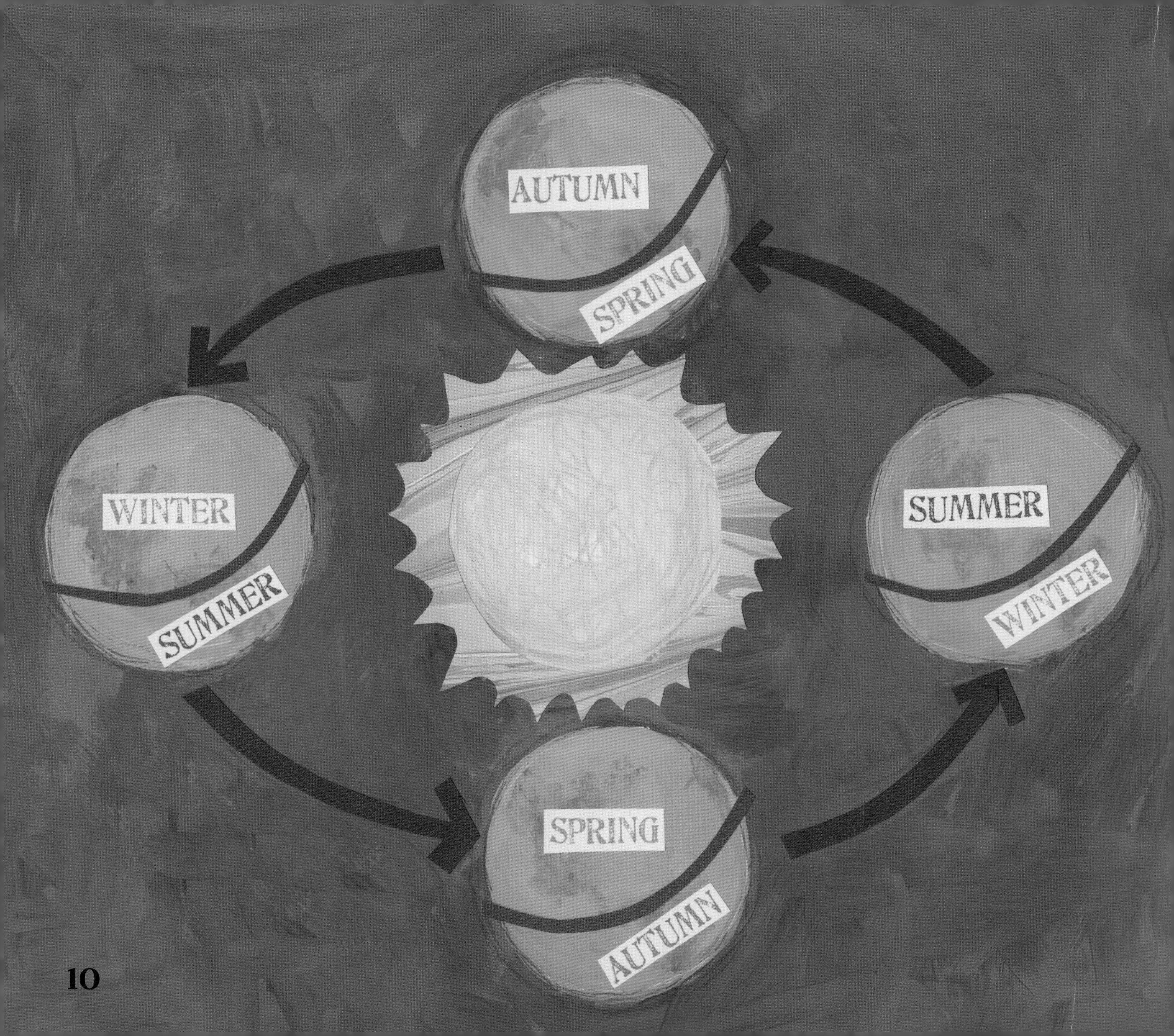

AUTUMN

SPRING

WINTER

SUMMER

SUMMER

WINTER

SPRING

AUTUMN

10

Summer lasts from June until September.
Unless you live below the **equator**!
Then summer is from December until March.

What's It Like Out?

In summer, it is hot!
The days are longer.

Sometimes it storms during the summer.
Other times there are **droughts**.

14

15

What Do They Do?

In summer, plants grow.
Crops ripen and flowers bloom.
Animals look for food and try to stay cool.

16

18

Most people do not go to school during the summer.
They take vacations and travel.

People also spend more time outdoors.
They swim, build sand castles, and have fun.
Soon, it will be autumn!
Do you know what will happen then?

21

Seasons

January Winter

February Winter

March Winter Spring

April Spring

May Spring

June Spring Summer

Summer Activities

Go Swimming

Pick Flowers

See a Parade

Go for a Walk

Go Biking

Watch Fireworks

Visit a Zoo

Web Sites

To learn more about the seasons, visit ABDO Group online. Web sites about the seasons are featured on our Book Links page. These links are routinely monitored and updated to provide the most current information available.

www.abdopublishing.com

Glossary

drought - (DRAUT) a long period of dry weather.

equator - an imaginary circle around the middle of Earth. It splits Earth into two equal parts.

summer solstice - (SUH-mer SAHL-stehs) the longest day of the year. The summer solstice usually occurs on June 20 or 21.

temperature - (TEHM-puhr-chur) the measured level of hot or cold.

Index

For Every
Individual...

Renew by Phone
269-5222

Renew on the Web
www.indypl.org

For General Library Information
please call 275-4100